UZZIAH MUST DIE

UZZIAH MUST DIE

STEPHEN ADESEMUYI

PARTRIDGE
A Penguin Random House Company

To order additional copies of this book, contact
Toll Free 0800 990 914 (South Africa)
+44 20 3014 3997 (outside South Africa)
orders.africa@partridgepublishing.com

www.partridgepublishing.com/africa

TABLE OF CONTENTS

List of previously published books by same author (Also by Stephen Adesemuyi):
1. Throw Your NET into the SEA.
2. The Secrets About Samuel.
3. Who is Your God?

"To heaven-minded people"

PREFACE

The biblical record of prophet Isaiah in the book of Isaiah 6:1 that **"In the year that king Uzziah died I saw also the Lord sitting upon a throne, high and lifted up, and his train filled the temple"** has generated a common prayer in many Christian gatherings, crusades and revivals that **'let the Uzziah of my life die'**. Many people see Uzziah as the enemy of their lives, and as somebody who will not allow them to see the glory of God unless, he gets out of the way. Is this view about Uzziah correct? Is Uzziah that kind of blockage to progress, to vision, to ambition, to success and to breakthrough? Of course, it could be and it may not. There is, therefore, the need to x-ray the life of Uzziah for who he is and what he stands for. It is only then we can justify, or otherwise, the rationality of the prayer *'Uzziah must die'*.

Summarily, Uzziah was the king of Judah in the time of prophet Isaiah. His father was Amasiah. He began to reign at the young age of sixteen years. He sought the Lord at the beginning of his reign and the Lord prospered him. Later, when he became strong, his heart was lifted up to his destruction. He intruded into the priesthood office to burn incense and for this, the Lord smote him with leprosy and he remained a leper for the rest of his life.

The life of king Uzziah is worthy of our study as Christians and should be for our divine lessons and instructions.

INTRODUCTION

Times without number, I have read the fascinating story of Uzziah the king of Judah in the Bible. I have also gone through a couple of books and listened to some sermons on this same great king. As a minister of the word of God, I have preached on Uzziah and referred to both his strength and weaknesses. The combination of all these first deceived me to assume that there was nothing new to see and learn in this book, UZZIAH MUST DIE.

As I began to read however, my wrong assumptions dissolved. I had to vomit my pride, burry my past knowledge and then open my heart to receive from the Holy Spirit through the lessons brought to light in this book you are holding in your hands. Indeed, I was blessed and I know you too will, without doubt, receive warnings and instructions that will make you both better Christian and a more efficient co-labourer with God in His vineyard. I recommend this book as a must read for every young convert and old disciple alike. Both the young ministers and experienced ones will find it invaluable as they run to fulfill their call into ministry.

Sola Oki
Evangelist, Author and President;
Liberation Time Evangelistic Ministry
Akure, Nigeria.

ACKNOWLEDGEMENT

I give God the glory for all the information and revelations in this book and for the liberation of every oppressed soul that shall encounter this book.

Thanks to the entire members of The Redeem Christian Church of God and particularly to Pastor E. A. Adeboye, the General Overseer of RCCG, whose wide and accommodating umbrella shielded me from the hot baking sun.

My unalloyed appreciation also goes to all the people whose spiritual armory and counseling have contributed to my spiritual progress. Special among them are Pastor and Pastor (Mrs) Ogunode, Pastor and Pastor (Mrs) D. A. Adeleye and Pastor Nasiru Ayodele all of RCCG, Pastor A. F. Akande of End Time Trumpeters Evangelical Ministries, Prophet I. B. Oke of Miracle Voice of Christ Evangelistic Ministries (MIVOCEM). Others include Reverend D. S. Daramola of Living Christ Bible Assembly, Reverend Taiwo Akeredolu and Bishop Wale Aiyegbusi of Flame of Fire Ministries, Oba-Akoko.

I also want to recognize with gratitude, the outstanding contribution of my darling wife Mrs Faith Adesemuyi and all my God-given children. They provided the necessary peaceful and comfortable atmosphere for this work.

A special gratitude also goes to Evangelist Sola Oki for painstakingly going through the manuscript and making necessary corrections and suggestions that led to the success of this book. His own book titled '**Praying Like Jesus**' has been and will continue to be a source of encouragement for me and I strongly recommend it to all people too.

This piece shall not be complete if I fail to mention the good role played by the family of Pastor and Pastor (Mrs) Adigun who came into my life when I reached a crossroad. Thank you and God bless.

Finally, I thank the Management and staff of Ondo State Water Corporation for giving me the opportunity to minister in their midst. To you all I express my sincere gratitude and God bless.

CHAPTER ONE

A GOOD START

Uzziah was the son of Amaziah, king of Judah. He was sixteen years old when the royal mantle fell upon his shoulder and he reigned in Judah for fifty-two years – 2Chronicles 26:1.
At that 16 years of age, Uzziah was probably too young to have the wisdom, knowledge, understanding, vision and strength needed for such exalted position and to rule successfully a great and God's nation like Israel that comprised of old men with grey hairs and different mindsets. This big challenge made Uzziah to seek the Lord as soon as he mounted the throne. Solomon in his own case asked the Lord for wisdom and understanding to rule the people of Israel. Usually, people below 18 years of age are considered not ripe enough for such sensitive leadership positions in some parts of the world.

A Good Start with the Lord.

What do you do when you face such a big challenge? Interestingly, Uzziah did what was right in the sight of the Lord -'*he sought the Lord*'.

> *"And he did that which was right in the sight of the Lord, according to all that his father Amaziah did. And he sought God in the days of Zechariah, who had understanding in the visions of God: and as long as he sought the LORD, God made him to prosper"* – 2 Chronicles 26:4-5.

Seeking the Lord was indeed a good start and a right step in the right direction for king Uzziah because the Lord rewarded him with prosperity. It is a good thing to start one's life endeavour, journey, academics, business, marriage and other issues of life with the Lord. The Bible enjoins us to commit our ways to the Lord who will direct our path and make crooked path straight – Psalm 37:5; Isaiah 45:2.
Uzziah sought the Lord who is the custodian of all good things of life including wisdom, knowledge and understanding and who gives every good and perfect gift to all men liberally and upbraids not – James 1:5.

He sought the Lord who is the supreme King of the universe: the immortal, the invisible, and the only wise; the Lord who knows the heart of the people over whom he was about to reign. What a good way to start his reign!

He sought the Lord who made him the firstborn in the family, who spared his life to succeed his father, and who did not allow him to be consumed by the hot polygamous war that customarily characterized royal homes.

Uzziah did not seek the gods and goddesses of the land, the necromancers, witch doctors or traditional priests for consultation, but sought the Lord of heaven and earth, the Ancient of Days, who is greater than any kingmaker or goddess of the land.

It is pertinent to mention here that seeking the Lord is a sign of respect for God and recognition of the supremacy and superiority of the Almighty God and the Lord considered it as a right action for king Uzziah.

Secondly, **Uzziah sought God in the right direction**. Whoever seeks God in the proper way shall find Him: *"and ye shall seek me and find me, when you shall seek me with all your heart. And I will be found of you, thus saith the Lord"* – Jeremiah 29: 13, 14.

Young in age and inexperienced in spiritual matters, king Uzziah sought the Lord *'in the days of Zechariah, who had understanding in the visions of God'* – 2 Chronicles 26:5. Zechariah was a true prophet of God who had understanding in the visions of God. Whatever Uzziah needed from God, he was humble enough to go through the prophet of God. Despite the existing traditions in the land, king Uzziah recognized the superiority of spirituality over traditionalism.

Whom Do You Seek?

Today, when people get to a position of authority of this nature, they seek different things for different purposes. While some seek political godfathers, false spiritualists and secret societies for refuge, support and direction, others rely on their personal ability, self-acquired knowledge and theoretical principles from books. All these could only offer temporary helps (if any) in any critical situation but the end is not always palatable.

Can anyone play the role and place of God the Almighty - the all-knowing, all-time visionary and the Master Planner of all generations? No one can play God in another man's life, not even the Presidents of the most technologically developed nations of the world! Only God has the ability and capability to place a person in position, empower him and sustain him in that position of power.

Unfortunately, among those that seek God, only few people seek Him for good purpose and for spiritual things that have eternal value. Others who claim to seek the Lord today sometimes do so for carnal purposes such as material things, riches and wealth, political and academic ambitions and positions that only have earthly value.

Ways of Seeking the Lord

The Bible lays down many proper ways of seeking the Lord. They include the following.

Through God's Prophets.

Seeking God through God's prophets, as Uzziah did, is the quickest way of knowing the mind of God concerning any particular situation. This is because prophets have the special gift of hearing and receiving secrets directly from God to provide solutions to the problems of the people. They are the mouthpieces of God. The Bible says, '*believe in the Lord your God, so shall ye be established; believe His prophets, so shall ye prosper*' – II Chronicles 20:20.

Prophets like Moses, Isaiah, Jeremiah, Ezekiel, Daniel, John the Baptist and a host of them were noted for bringing solutions to the problems of individuals and nations. Even today, God still speaks through the prophets to guide the people and solve their problems.

However, caution must be taken in the consultation of prophets today because the society is full of many false prophets and so-called spiritualists who mislead and deceive people with false visions, revelations and prophesy in this end time - 2 Peter 2:1 and 2 John 7.

Through the Word of God

Another way to seek the Lord is personal devotion to reading and meditating on the word of God – the Holy Bible. The word of God contains the mind, the will, the purpose, promise and covenant of God in all areas of life – marriage, business, finances, etc.

The word of God is settled in heaven concerning any matter and it is a lamp to the feet and a light to our path. It is quick, sharp and powerful ... and is a discerner of the thoughts and intents of the heart and all things are naked and opened unto it – Hebrews 4:12, 13. All one needs do is develop ability to study the word diligently, meditate on it, understand it, obey any instruction from it and apply it correctly to any situation. Like God told Joshua, we would make our ways prosperous and have good success if we stay in His word.

Through Fasting and Prayer

Another effective way of seeking God for direction and guidance is fasting and prayer. Prayer is communication with God in which God answers and gives specific direction. Fasting is the catalyst to prepare the altar of the heart for effective prayer. The two, when combined together, give our spirit easy access to the supernatural realm and afford us the power to solve intricate problems – Matthew 17:21

Great men in the Bible, and in our contemporary world, were people who made fasting and prayer their ways of life. Moses, Elijah, Daniel, Paul and Jesus are a few examples in the list of Bible heroes of prayer while many of the successful General Overseers in our society can be included in this list.

Through prayer, a person can know the mind of God concerning any issue, sometimes, through dreams, revelation, inspiration, etc. The Lord himself says; *"Then shall ye call upon me, and ye shall go and pray unto me, and I shall hearken unto you. And ye shall seek me, and find me, when you shall search for me with all your heart."* – Jeremiah 29:12-13. The promise of God is that when we pray, He will answer and show us great things – Jeremiah 33:3.

However, effective fasting and prayer involves a life of holiness and sacrifice, which many people cannot afford - Isaiah 58:3-14.

Through The Holy Spirit

In all the aforementioned ways of seeking the Lord, the Holy Spirit is the one who works things out for effective results. He is the activator of prayer for we know not how we ought to pray but the Holy Spirit helps us to pray – Romans 8:26. He is also the searcher of the deep things of God and revealer of the truth – I Corinthians 2:10.

It is certain, from above, that if one seeks the Lord in the proper way, one will find Him. Our Lord Jesus gives the assurance that if we ask, seek and knock we will receive answer - Mathew 7:7. God's words are yea and amen. His promises are sure if we meet all the conditions associated with them.

CHAPTER TWO

THE GREAT REWARD

G od is the Rewarder of those who diligently seek Him – Hebrews 11:6. Whoever trusts in God shall not be put to shame. King Uzziah sought the Lord the right way and the Lord rewarded him with prosperity – 2 Chronicles 26:5.

"And he sought God in the days of Zechariah, who had understanding in the visions of God: and as long as he sought the Lord, God made him to prosper".

Power or position does not guarantee prosperity until one involves God in it – Romans 9:16. Anything minus God is nothing. King Uzziah involved God in his royal position and *'God made him to prosper'*. Only God can prosper a person without adding sorrow to it. Therefore, prosperity, success or breakthrough is a matter of *divine connection* rather than *human connection.*

ANYTHING MINUS GOD IS NOTHING

The Bible states that as strong as the lion is, the young lion still lacks and suffers hunger, but *'they that seek the Lord shall not lack any good thing'* – Psalm 34:10. God sure has some good packages to give to those who diligently and successfully seek and find Him. He will save, bless, redeem, deliver and prosper them.

The Reward of Seeking God

Definitely, there is reward for whatever anybody does. There is a reward for every praise and worship, prayer, fasting, night vigil, evangelism, tithe, offering and giving that anyone does. There is also a reward for laziness, disobedience and deception. The Bible says whatsoever a man sows, that he shall reap and therefore charges us not to be weary in well doing for in due season we shall reap, if we faint not – Galatians 6:7, 9. Seeking the Lord is a well doing and it attracts good rewards some of which are stated below.

Recovery

Seeking the Lord will bring about recovery of all that has been lost – materials, fortune, opportunities and time. For example, David sought the Lord *in prayer* when the Amalekites raided his possession at Ziklag and God made him to pursue, to overtake and to recover all that was lost to the enemies – 1 Samuel 30:8 -19.

> *"And David enquired at the LORD, saying, Shall I pursue after this troop? shall I overtake them? And he answered him, Pursue: for thou shalt surely overtake them, and without fail recover all"*
> And <u>David recovered all</u> that the Amalekites had carried away: and David rescued his two wives (emphasis mine).

Divine Favour

Seeking the Lord wholeheartedly attracts divine favour. Esther sought the Lord in *fasting and prayer* for three days and she went to the king at the un-appointed time only to receive favour instead of death in the sight of the king – Esther 4:16 - 5:2.

> *"Go, gather together all the Jews that are present in Shushan, and fast ye for me …. And it was so, when the king saw Esther the queen standing in the court, that she obtained favour in his sight…"*

Deliverance

A person who seeks the Lord enjoys deliverance from sin, enemies or trouble. For example, when the early church was persecuted and Peter was imprisoned, the church sought the Lord in a fervent *all-night prayer* and the angel of the Lord delivered Peter from the prison – Acts. 12:5-10. In addition, the same angel of the Lord smote king Herod to death after which the gospel grew and multiplied – Acts 12:21-24.

Prosperity

In the case of king Uzziah, the Lord prospered him by causing the Ammorites to bring gifts to the king. He became rich in cattle and vineyards and God made him so popular such that Uzziah's name was a kind of a visa to enter the land of Egypt – 2 Chronicles 26:8.

> *"And the Ammonites gave gifts to Uzziah: and his name spread abroad even to the entering in of Egypt; for he strengthened himself exceedingly".*

Victory

Another benefit for seeking the Lord is to enjoy divine victory. King Uzziah gained and enjoyed divine victory and security over his enemies that surrounded him – the Philistines, Arabians and Ammonites – 2 Chronicles 26:6-8. The king *"had a host of fighting men, that went out to war by bands – people that made war with mighty power, to help the king against the enemy"* – 2Chronicles 26: 11, 13.

Jehoshaphat sought the Lord *in fasting and prayer* and the Lord gave him victory over all his enemies: the Moabites, Ammonites and people from mount Seir - 2 Chronicles 20:3, 22-23.

Rest

With divine victory over sin or the enemy, there will be rest and peace of mind in the home and city. King Jehoshaphat had rest in his territory because of seeking the face of God – 2 Chronicles 20:29-30.

> *"And the fear of God was on all the kingdoms of those countries, when they had heard that the LORD fought against the enemies of Israel.*
> *So the realm of Jehoshaphat was quiet: for his God gave him rest round about".*

Similarly, Samuel sought God in prayer when the Philistines gathered in battle against Israel and God gave the Israelites territorial peace and victory over their enemies - 1Samuel 7:10-13.

How long does the Reward Last?

Yes, the Lord prospered king Uzziah for seeking Him. However, the prosperity, victory, protection and other benefits enjoyed by the king continued *'as long as he sought the Lord'* - 2 Chronicles 26:5.

There is a lesson to learn here. God is the source of our life – power, wealth and blessing. Therefore, He requires us to have total and all-day, all-time and all-season fellowship with Him for continuity of supply. His covenant and promises are conditional and last as long as we keep to our own parts. Seeking God should be an all-time affair. The moment one stops to seek Him, He will also stop his own response toward one. Whenever one stops seeking God, then one starts dying. This is because when a tree stops growing, it starts to wither and to die.

In a nutshell, the reward of seeking God will last as long as there is **continuity**:

Continuity in **fellowship** with God, the source of our supply;
Continuity with **the Giver of the Gifts**;
Continuity in our **faith and trust** in the Lord;
Continuity in our **obedience** to God;
Continuity in our **services** to God.

> # WHENEVER ONE STOPS SEEKING GOD, ONE STARTS DYING

How About You?

This is exactly the situation with many people today. When you first gave your life to Jesus, you were young and naive but very fervent, thirsty and eager for the things of God. You were close to your pastors and Sunday School Teachers for counseling and guidance. You were married to your Bible, and were punctual and regular at Bible Studies and other fellowship activities. This is because you were still young, and you never knew the way, hence you sought the Lord.

Likewise, when you first started your ministry or became a new member of the church, you sought the Lord with all your strength. As a young minister, you used to go from house to house for evangelism, doing visitation of new converts and organizing several crusades to draw many souls to the Lord. You paid your tithes correctly and as at when due, gave offerings always with joy. Giving to the brethren and to the work of God was never a burden to you.

In addition, the word of God was so precious to you that you would make sure you read the Bible before you took your breakfast. No sleeping or wandering about during sermon but you listened attentively. You were obedient, respectful and humble. In other words, you had a strong *'first love'* for the Lord – Revelation 2: 4.

Furthermore, as a young Christian, you never prayed alone because of your inexperience in spiritual things, but you engaged the services of prayer warriors and prayer partners to tackle knotty problems. Like Uzziah, you *'had a host of fighting men, that went out to war by bands – people that made war with mighty power, to help the king against the enemy'*.

Like Uzziah equipped his entire warriors with shields, spears, helmets, habergeons, bows and slings, you put on the whole armour of God: loins of truth, breastplate of righteousness, shoes of evangelism, shields of faith, helmets of salvation, sword of the Spirit (Word of God) and prayers whereby you were able to withstand the evil days – Ephesians 6:10-18.

All these spiritual activities undoubtedly made you to grow and become strong in the Lord and in the power of His might: strong in faith, in prayer and in the knowledge of the word. The Lord has been faithful too. He has eventually prospered you and blessed you with multiple blessings: spiritual, financial, material and matrimonial.

Note that all these and many more benefits you will continue to enjoy *as long as you seek and walk with the Lord.* What happens if the person enjoying these benefits suddenly stops to seek God? All the benefits will also stop!

CHAPTER THREE

THE TURNING POINT

It is a pity that man sometimes abuses the provisions of God. The Bible affirms that God's provisions (blessing) make one rich and add no sorrow – Proverbs 10:22. Provisions like wealth, position and power should give us positive turning points in life by changing our status from bad to good and turning our hearts towards God.

Turning points are unavoidable in life but there is need to watch which way one is turning to. Positive turning point is good, like a *sinner* becoming a *saint* it is a bad turning point for a saint turning a sinner - Ezekiel 18:21.

Uzziah's Turning Point

It is unfortunate to know that after Uzziah reached the peak of his career as a king, he experienced a negative turning point by becoming a leper. What could be responsible for this bad turning point?

One: Pride

One major cause of king Uzziah's negative turning point is *pride*. The Bible says that *"his heart was lifted up to his destruction: for he transgressed against the Lord his God, and went into the temple of the Lord to burn incense upon the altar of incense" – 2 Chronicles 26: 16. (underlined mine for emphasis)*

Pride is a common phenomenon which has destroyed many lives, punctured many beautiful dreams and truncated many destinies. It is therefore, necessary to expatiate on it a little.

Pride is an attitude of self-exaltation, self-importance, self-advertisement, self-recognition or self-exaggeration. It is an act of overrating oneself than the reality. Pride is pictorial of a peacock or turkey bird, which spreads its tail feathers wide apart to make it look bigger than its size.

Pride is a symptom of madness that makes a person feel wise in his own eyes, even wiser than any other person just like a lunatic does. Pride will not allow its victim to see his true size and colour or to listen to or accept other people's advice, however good it may seem. In African's saying, pride is referred to as '*only I, only I*'.

Causes of Pride

The Bible says, *"But when he became strong, his heart was lifted up to destruction"* – II Chronicles 26:16. Uzziah became strong in power, authority, wealth and position and that was responsible for his sharp and sudden turning point

Position, Power and Authority

Power, they say, corrupts and absolute power corrupts absolutely. Power could be intoxicating more than wine. It requires the grace of God to keep one's desire, thoughts and actions under proper control and to avoid misuse of power once obtained. Power pushes. It has pushed many people to die a shameful death or to commit costly and irreversible mistakes that have led to the downfall of great men of history.

Kings like Pharaoh, Ahab, Sennacherib and Herod perished because of pride engineered and fueled by power. Satan also lost his heavenly position due to pride fuelled by pursuit of power. However, we find some powerful kings and great servants of God who are humble with their power and have been of benefits to the people.

Position of authority can also lead to pride. Many people after mounting the throne of authority would become big men who sit in glass houses, drive in tinted glass cars, and would no longer be approachable to the common masses.

Money

This is the most dangerous fuel of pride. It is the most effective determinant factor to reckon with in the pursuant of power and position. It is the yardstick for measuring the status, prosperity and the purchasing power of any man in the society. For example, every achievement that made king Uzziah strong in his kingdom was a factor of money. The provision of weapons for his army and the financing of various battles all cost money – 2 Chronicles 26:11-15.

With money on hands, there is usually a high tendency for a person to fall victim of pride. Just like wine, money intoxicates. God knows about this problem and he has cautioned us against the love of money.

"Beware that thou forget not the Lord thy God, in not keeping his commandments. Lest thou when thou hast eaten and art full…and thy silver and gold is multiplied, and all that thou hast is multiplied. Then thine heart be lifted up, and thou forget the Lord your God, which brought thee forth out of the land of Egypt, from the house of bondage" – Deuteronomy 8:11-15.

The Dangers of Pride

Pride is a great sin before the Lord and like other sins; its consequences are damn too fatal. It costs its victim to miss heaven and to end up in deep pit of destruction. Secondly, God hates pride and the proud and the following Scriptures should send enough warning signals to us.

- *Pride goeth before a destruction, and an haughty spirit before a fall* – Proverbs 16:18.
- *The Lord will destroy the house of the proud* – Proverbs 15:25.
- *Every one that is proud in heart is an abomination to the Lord: though hand joined in hand, he shall not be unpunished* – Proverbs 16:5.
- *God resisteth the proud, but giveth grace unto the humble* – James 4:6.
- *And he that humble himself shall be exalted* – Matthew 23:12.
- *Humble yourselves therefore under the mighty hand of God, that He may exalt you in due time* – 1Peter 5:6.

From above, one can see that king Uzziah who once enjoyed fame and prosperity from the Lord later allowed pride of fame, position, power and prosperity to ruin his life beyond recovery.

Are You a Victim of Pride?

Two: Forsaking God

Another reason for the negative turning point is that king Uzziah probably stopped seeking the Lord at a particular point in life. The Bible says *'and he sought God in the days of Zechariah, who had understanding in the visions of God: and as long as he sought the Lord God made him to prosper'* - 2 Chronicles 26:5.

The phrase *"as long as he sought the Lord,"* suggests that the king sought God for a period - in the days of prophet Zechariah - but later forsook God when the prophet was no more alive. The king shifted his focus from *'God'* to *'self'* and from the *'Provider'* to the *'provision'*. He began to rely on his own strength, power, wealth, wisdom, military capability and position, forgetting that the arm of flesh would fail a man.

Three: Hereditary Problem

It is common for a child to resemble his parents not only in good virtues like facial appearances, character, talk, walk and way of dressing but also in vices such as pride, anger, fighting, stubbornness, fornication as found among some groups of people, families, tribes, cultures and religion.

The Bible recorded that king Uzziah did that which was right in the sight of the Lord, *according to all that his father did.* The clause, *'according to all that his father did,'* should be viewed symbolically as it was used for three successive kings in the royal linage namely; Joash (2 Chronicles 24:2), Amaziah (2 Kings 14:3) and Uzziah (2 Chronicles 26:4). This looks like hereditary problem because Joash was the father of Amaziah and Amaziah was the father of Uzziah.

Apart from the right things they did in the sight of the Lord, some bad traits were common to these three successive kings namely; pride, stubbornness, disobedience, anger and murder.

For example, in 2 Chronicles 25:17, king Amaziah became *proud* after his victory over the Edomites and challenged Joash, the king of Israel, to fight. He became *angry* at the warning of the prophet of God, went ahead with the fight and this caused great *murder* among the people– 2 Chronicles 25:16-20.

In the same manner, Joash the father of Amaziah forsook God to serve idols after the death of Jehoiada the priest, *disobeyed* the prophets God sent to warn the people against their transgression and in his *anger,* he *murdered* Zechariah the son of Jehoiada the priest - 2 Chronicles 24:18-22.

Similarly, king Uzziah became a victim of *anger, pride* and *disobedience* (refusal to heed warning and advice of the men of God). Perhaps, king Uzziah would have *murdered* the priests who challenged him if God had not stricken him with leprosy on time!

It is therefore right to conclude that Uzziah inherited anger, pride and stubbornness, resisting, harassing, stoning and killing of the prophets and priests of God in the royal linage. All these habits can cause a negative turning point for a man in life!

Four: Ancestral Spirit

It is worthy to note that there was a good thing pertaining to king David in the royal family for the above-mentioned kings to inherit but they chose to follow the evils of other predecessors. According to 2 Kings 14: 3, Amaziah did all things according to Joash his father but *yet not like David his father*.

Transfer of evil traits from predecessors to successors is usually the work of ancestral spirit - an evil spirit dominant and in control of a family or genealogy. The spirit causes a child to have an evil resemblance of the parents. This is the reason some believers still experience intermittent manifestation of the old traditional nature after confessing Jesus Christ as Lord and Saviour. This is evil resemblance of highest order!

What did you inherit from your biological and spiritual parents?

Four: Tradition

The clause *'according to his father'* may refer to the royal tradition of the land. Traditions of the people are powerful and are difficult to uproot. King Uzziah would need to preserve the tradition, especially the high places, because *'the people had not prepared their hearts unto the God of their fathers'* - 2Chronicles 20:33. The truth is that tradition gives its adherents stubborn and proud heart against the Lord.

Can two walk together except they agree? – Amos 3:3. The idea of king Uzziah seeking the Lord while his subjects worship idols could not have worked together easily. The danger of such co-existence is that one day; the evil majority side is likely to buy over the righteous minority. That was what probably happened to Uzziah. The pressure of the traditional group eventually overpowered him.

Do you allow your children to go to cinema house while you go to church? There is tendency of spiritual pollution. Be careful, danger is looming ahead.

CHAPTER FOUR

DIVINE BOUNDARY AND DIVINE PLACEMENT

There is a purpose for everything God created and to fulfill that purpose, God located everything in its proper place and position. The sun, the moon and the stars are positioned in the sky to give lights to the earth at specific times. It will be abnormal for the sun to move from the sky to the ground or to give its light in the night!

Likewise, everybody has a place or position to occupy and a purpose to fulfill at one time or the other. Kings, Governors, Presidents and political leaders are in positions of authority over the natural affairs of the people while priests and other spiritual leaders are ordained to run the spiritual affairs of the people. In essence, there is a place for the king and a place for the priest and each leader operates within a set boundary limit. The place for the king is the Palace while Sanctuary is the place reserved for the priest.

> # THERE IS A PLACE FOR THE KING AND A PLACE FOR THE PRIEST.

Each leadership position has its own peculiar characteristics, requirements, skill acquisitions, rules and ethics to enhance high performance and efficiency. Therefore, to dabble into another man's duty without the required technical or spiritual knowledge is to commit a high-level blunder.

The king is the traditional head of the people, enthroned according to some traditional rites and amidst various religions, traditions, taboos and superstitions. He has a royal apparel, crown on his head, beads on his neck, scepter in his hand and a throne in the palace that distinguishes him from his chiefs and other people. The king is customarily polygamous and he is often referred to as the *'husband of the town'*.

On the other hand, Priests are spiritual leaders ordained of God for different types of work in the vineyard at specific periods and, many at times, at specific locations. They are guided by moral and spiritual laws. For example, they must be *'husband of one wife'* and *'must not be given to wine, greed or fight'* - 1Timothy 3:1-5. Furthermore, priests do undergo some practical trainings and spiritual purification processes concerning the services at the sanctuary.

The purification process of priests today involves new birth experience, sanctification experience through the word of God, prayer and Holy Ghost. Burning of incense at the sanctuary is tantamount to preaching and prayer, series of Bible studies, quiet time, fasting, preparation of sermon notes and receiving inspiration, revelation and anointing before he finally comes to the altar to minister.

Crossing Divine Boundary

Apart from pride, the second problem king Uzziah had was that *he crossed his royal boundary* to perform the priest's sacred duty of burning incense! As mentioned above, the place of the king is the palace while that of the Priest is the sanctuary, the Church. There is therefore a boundary limit for each of them. The king's action to cross the boundary limits amounted to violation of divine order and authority and it attracted grave consequences.

Dangers of Crossing Ones Boundary

The following dangers can arise from crossing one's divine assignment to another without divine instruction and proper preparation.

Defilement

When a person crosses his duty boundary to another without divine revelation or instruction, his original placement will suffer negligence while the new one will suffer defilement. For example, Uzziah neglected his royal duty to perform priesthood duty for which he was not ordained to do, thereby defiling the altar. God regards an un-authorized sacrifice on the holy altar as strange fire and visits such with grave consequences.

The Bible prescribes that only people with clean hands and pure hearts shall ascend the hill of the Lord and stand in His holy place - Psalms 24:3-4. Jesus, the head of the Church, notably cleansed the temple of material and spiritual pollution at Jerusalem – Matthew 21:12.

Unfortunately, many people still defile the sanctuary today with impunity and there seems to be no instant or physical consequences upon the defilers. Many buying, selling, and money exchange activities have defiled an originally designed '*house of God*' and '*house of prayer*'. Promiscuous acts among members, tithes and offerings from unclean sources, false prophecies, lies and curses are acts of defilement to the sanctuary. All these things should attract instant judgment like that of Uzziah but for the tender mercy of God! However, the penalty awaits them later in life if they fail to repent.

War

Everybody belongs to one territory or another. Every territory has its own security outfits against territorial invasion, boundary encroachment, external aggression and immigration. The security outfit of a particular territory could be as strong and tight as the wall of Jericho and it would take a war to break through it. For example, it took Joshua a serious battle to cross over the territorial boundaries of the Canaanites before he could possess the Promised Land.

Similarly, the house of God has its own security outfit - angels are always on guard and the word of God is readily available to guide peaceful co-existence of members. Despite this, many churches today are facing serious battles of segregation, sectionalism, rancor and division because false doctrines, worldliness, fashion, culture have crossed over their boundaries into the church.

Likewise, many homes are facing civil wars because strange men and women have crossed over to their legitimate marital territories. One good example was king David who crossed his marital boundary to commit adultery with Uriah's wife and for that reason, the sword of battle never departed from his home – 2 Samuel 12:10. The life battle you are facing today may be the result of the boundary you or/and your ancestors have crossed. Check your life!

Physical Death

According to the Law of Moses, only the Levites were ordained to come near the sanctuary, any other person would die. The Lord said to Moses,

> "*Therefore, thou and thy sons with thee shall keep your priest's office for everything of the altar, and within the veil; and ye shall serve: I have given your priest's office unto you as a service of gift: **and the stranger that cometh nigh shall be put to death**" – Numbers 18: 7.*

33

In working contrary to above injunction, Uza (not a Levite) touched the ark of God un-authorized and dropped dead while King Uzziah (a non-priest) performed priesthood sacrifice outside his royal function and he became a leper.

Even sanctuary workers must be cautious not to be like Nadab and Abihu (sons of Aaron) who offered strange fire to the Lord and died in the process - Leviticus 10:1-2. *"And Nadab and Abihu, the sons of Aaron, ... offered strange fire before the LORD, which he commanded them not. And there went out fire from the LORD, and devoured them, and they died before the LORD".*

Spiritual Death

Sometimes, crossing of boundary leads to spiritual death. Many *so-called* and *self-called* ministers of God who serve at the sanctuary have ended up in spiritual mortuary! Many have lost their power, anointing and vision though they think they are still alive but they are spiritually dead – Revelation 3: 1.

Like king Saul confessed, God does not talk to them anymore either by dream, vision or revelation - 1 Samuel 28:15. They only say '*thus says the Lord*' when God has not spoken. In other to cover up their incompetence, they go to the mediums to obtain evil powers to do the work of the sanctuary. God cannot be deceived. As it was for Uzziah, their punishment, their own type of leprosy, is beside the altar which they have polluted, waiting to smite them!

Curses and Diseases

There is possibility of a curse and disease for anybody who breaks a spiritual law, ignorance notwithstanding. King Uzziah crossed his boundary and contacted leprosy disease. Gehazi contravened the order of Prophet Elisha and he was cursed and became a leper for the rest of his life.

Plenty of the self-called ministers of God today have broken the sanctity order of the church and have therefore become sick, diseased and cursed in one way or the other while some have their own leprosy awaiting them at the altar.

Stay Within Your Boundary

The Lord gives diverse spiritual gifts to every individual to function well in the vineyard. These gifts are given according to a certain measure of grace and faith. The Bible advises us to *wait on our own gifts* and operate them with *the proportion of faith, simplicity, diligence and cheerfulness.*

> *"Having then gifts **differing according to the grace that is given to us**, Whether prophecy, let us prophesy **according to the proportion of faith;** Or ministering, **let us wait on our ministering;** Or he that teacheth, on teaching; Or he that exhorteth, on exhortation; He that giveth, **let him do it with simplicity;** He that ruleth, **with diligence;** He that showeth mercy, **with cheerfulness"** –* Romans 12:6-8

Unfortunately, some have abandoned their callings, visions, gifts and ministries to copy another man's vision and ministry. In the process, they have lost their originality and are no longer fit for the use of the Master.

Priests should identify their individual divine callings and places of assignment and stay within them. Only then can they enjoy God's provision of *'touch not my anointed and do my prophet no evil'.*

Peter and Paul were examples of ministers who stayed within their ministerial boundaries and they prospered in their ministries. Today, we read their epistles as evidence of their fulfilled life. Likewise, Joshua operated within a specific *physical boundary* of the land he was about to inherit as well as the *spiritual boundary* of a given book of the law and the promises of possession, protection and victory came to fulfillment – Joshua (1:4-8).

There are also some specific marriage boundaries for believers. These include; *'one man, one wife'* (Matthew 19:4-9), *'flee fornication and adultery'* (1Corinthians 6:18), and *'love and submission to one another'* (Ephesians 5:21-28). Those who stay within these boundaries have blessings; peace and comfort in their marriages while those who go outside them do bear the grave consequences.

CHAPTER FIVE

THE HIGH COST OF STUBBORNNESS

God does not usually descend on any sinner with an immediate judgment without first giving him several warnings and chances to repent and live – Ezekiel 18:23. However, when the person proves stubborn and fails to yield to the warnings, then God's judgment will come down on him.

For example, God warned king Pharaoh with ten plagues before the final judgment fell on him at the Red Sea due to Pharaoh's stubbornness. Likewise, Jesus forewarned the repercussion of his betrayal but Judas Iscariot chose not to heed the warning because of his stubbornness and he perished for it – Luke 22:20-22.

The Longsuffering of God

God is rich in mercy and slow to anger. He is good to the righteous and the wicked peradventure, the wicked will change his ways someday. The delay in passing judgment immediately a man sins and the opportunity given to amend his ways marks the longsuffering of God.

The Bible tells us that God loves man and He is therefore patient with a sinner because He does not want anybody to perish:

> "The Lord is not slack concerning his promise, as some men count slackness; but is longsuffering to us-ward, not willing that any should perish, but that all should come to repentance" - 2 Peter 3:9.
> "For God so loved the world, that he gave his only begotten Son, that whosoever believeth in him should not perish, but have everlasting life"- John 3:16-18.

However, there is a timeframe for every sinner to come unto repentance. The door of salvation is open when a man is still alive but closes when death comes. Therefore, the Bible says that the day of salvation should be today, even now – now that you are still breathing.

"For he saith, I have heard thee in a time accepted, and in the day of salvation have I succoured thee: behold, now is the accepted time; behold, <u>*now is the day of salvation"*</u> - 2Corinthians 6:2.

Fortunately, the Lord's invitation is still open as He knocks at the door of your heart again saying;

"Behold, I stand at the door, and knock: if any man hear my voice, and open the door, I will come in to him, and will sup with him, and he with me" - Revelation 3:20. You are therefore advised to open the door of your heart for the Lord to come inside and do not try to break the elastic limit of God's patience by your stubbornness.

STUBBORNNESS BREAKS THE ELASTIC LIMIT OF GOD'S LONGSUFFERING

The Steps of Stubbornness

God knew the gravity of the trespasses king Uzziah was about to commit and He therefore sent *eighty-one valiant priests* (fourscore plus Azariah the high priest) to withstand him (put up a resistance) and prevent him from committing the sin but the king chose not to listen. Instead, he became angry with the priests and stubbornly held on to the censer, still determined to carry out his illegal and un-ordained action until judgment came upon him from the altar. In order to appreciate the longsuffering of God in the case under study let us analyze the stubbornness of king Uzziah!

The Wrong Action

Is God not merciful and patient enough with sinners? The **censer** and the **incense** are sacred vessels, already consecrated for use in the sanctuary by holy, pure, clean and ordained men and not with ordinary men with unclean hands.

"Depart ye, depart ye, go ye out from thence, touch no unclean thing; go ye out of the midst of her, be ye clean, that bear the vessels of the Lord" – Isaiah 52:11.

King Uzziah was neither consecrated nor ordained to serve at the sanctuary. He was not cleansed from the traditional rituals of the palace and from the mess of a polygamous family. Therefore, mere touching the holy vessels should have attracted immediate physical death penalty: *and the stranger that cometh nigh shall be put to death"* – Numbers 18: 7. Nevertheless, God exercised some patience with the king!

The Warnings

God took time and steps to warn the king. He sent the priests to show that the king's action was wrong, yet the king was too stubborn to listen. These steps are contained in the following context.

"And Azariah the priest went in after him, and with him fourscore priests of the LORD, that were valiant men:

And they withstood Uzziah the king, and said unto him, It appertaineth not unto thee, Uzziah, to burn incense unto the LORD, but to the priests the sons of Aaron, that are consecrated to burn incense: go out of the sanctuary; for thou hast trespassed; neither shall it be for thine honour from the LORD God" – 2 Chronicles 26:17-18.

First step of warning

God sent eighty-one valiant priests (not ordinary men) to withstand the king from going further in his action.

"And Azariah the priest went in after him, and with him fourscore priests of the LORD, that were valiant men... And they withstood Uzziah the king..."

Why sending eighty-one priests? God knew the seriousness of the action and its grave consequences. Each priest stood for one warning from the Lord because each of the priests carried God's anointing, power and message. The eighty-one priests combined power, anointing and message to prevent the king but the king remained stubborn. How often does God speak to us but we remain bent on our own ideas and actions!

Second step of warning

Besides, God made the king know it was not the duty of the king to do what he was about to do but the king did not listen.

"It appertaineth not unto thee, Uzziah, to burn incense unto the LORD".

Third step of warning

God made it clear that only the priests were qualified to perform that particular assignment and the king was never a priest.

"It appertaineth not unto thee, Uzziah, to burn incense unto the LORD, but to the priests the sons of Aaron".

Fourth step of warning

God told him that the spiritual condition of the people qualified to burn incense is 'consecration': "*but to the priests the sons of Aaron, that are consecrated to burn incense"*

Uzziah was initiated into the tradition of the land and was never consecrated to the things of altar of God.

Fifth step of warning

God told the king the result of his action that it would not be to his good: "*neither shall it be for thine honour from the LORD God".* What else did the king want to know or hear that God had not told him? Yet he proved stubborn!

Sixth step of warning

God told the king that such action amounted to trespass:

"Go out of the sanctuary; for thou hast trespassed".

The sanctuary is for the priests and it was a trespass for any other person not ordained to enter, however highly placed. Though Jesus Christ at the Calvary had removed the veil, yet sanctuary work is still reserved for the ministers of God. Unfortunately, many people are guilty of these offences today.

Seventh step of warning

There is always a final warning, the last warning after which judgment becomes inevitable. This was eventually the final warning for king Uzziah. God specifically told the king from the mouth of His priests to go out of the sanctuary: *"go out of the sanctuary; for thou hast trespassed".*

Uzziah should have heeded this last and final warning but he did not! He did not move a step; rather, he was trying to claim authority with God in God's own house!

There are also specific and final warnings in the Bible such as; *'flee fornication'* (1Corinthians 6:18), *'let anyone who calls the name of the Lord depart from iniquity'* (2 Timothy 2:19) **and** *'do not touch unclean thing ...'*(Isaiah 52:11). How much of these instructions do you know and obey?

The King's Stubborn Reaction

King Uzziah never saw reason with God and the priests despite all the above warnings. Even if the king could not see the invisible God, the huge number of the priests sent to him was enough to bring him down to his knees. Instead, he was stubborn; he refused to withdraw his action. Let us examine the king's reaction as contained in these Bible verses.

> *"Then Uzziah was wroth, and had a censer in his hand to burn incense: and while he was wroth with the priests, the leprosy even rose up in his forehead before the priests in the house of the LORD, from beside the incense altar"* - 2 Chronicles 26:19.

First Reaction: He Held On the Censer

King Uzziah held on to his action and position despite God's disapproval. Instead of dropping the censer, which is an indication of withdrawal from such action, the king held on to the censer, still bent on burning incense!

> *"Then Uzziah was wroth, and had a censer in his hand to burn incense..."*

The same is true today. Despite all the preaching and teachings against immorality, wickedness, murder, abortion, corruption and many other vices in the churches, many people still hold on to these sins. They believe that they must enjoy their lives, as they like. The Bible has this to say:

"But she that liveth in pleasure is dead while she liveth" - 1Timothy 5:6.

What evil are you holding on to: wickedness, lies, stealing, fornication, bribery or embezzlement? Evil belongs to the devil. Drop it, otherwise, like Uzziah who held on to what did not belong to him, you would **pay dearly for it**.

That strange woman you carry on your chest is like fire and she will burn you if you do not let her go. Proverbs 6:27-29 says; *"Can a man take fire in his bosom, and his clothes not be burned? Can one go upon hot coals, and his feet not be burned? So he that goeth in to his neighbour's wife; whosoever toucheth her shall not be innocent"*.

Perhaps, some people believe that with the level of civilization they can commit sin with impunity. For example, people commercialize fornication and adultery with the thought that the use of *'condom'* and other *'contraceptives'* would prevent unwanted pregnancies and make them to escape the infection of sexually transmitted diseases. That is fine. However, I hope that technology would make the condom thick enough to protect the people against the heat of hell fire, the shame and sufferings associated with breaking of God's commandment in the last day.

> # CONDOM MAY PROTECT AGAINST HIV/AIDS BUT CANNOT PROTECT AGAINST HELL FIRE!

Second Reaction: He Was Wrath

The king became angry with the priests.

"Then Uzziah was wroth, and had a censer in his hand to burn incense: and while he was wroth with the priests".

Human beings do make mistakes but God in His merciful and longsuffering nature will reveal these to us in several ways. The question is 'how do we react when God points out our sins and flaws'? Some people react with aggression, hatred and bitterness against our pastors or spiritual leaders, threatening to leave *his church* for him. The church of God now becomes *'his church'*.

Message of rebuke or correction may come from the pulpit or by prophecy. That is what the word of God should do in the lives of believers:

> *"All scripture is given by inspiration of God, and is profitable for doctrine, for reproof, for correction, for instruction in righteousness: that the man of God may be perfect, thoroughly furnished unto all good works"* - 2 Timothy 3:16.

The word of God is not a gladiator that is meant to entertain the hearers but it is a *hammer* and *fire* (Jeremiah 23:29) and *sword* (Hebrews 4:12). Therefore, when one is hit and cut by its sharp edges, or is burnt by its hot flame; the response should not be that of anger but of soberness and repentance so that God can show mercy and turn away His wrath and heal the wound created.

Anger would only worsen already bad situation. As for king Uzziah who was already intoxicated with pride, anger blindfolded him and he could not recognize the presence of the invisible and powerful God in the temple. He did not see the ministering angels stand by, waiting for instruction to strike him with leprosy. Like pride, anger is a destroyer of life, careers and destinies and leaders should avoid it like a plague.

The Cost of Stubbornness

The cost of stubbornness is usually high and sometimes unquantifiable. The consequences can also be seriously terrible and irreversible.

Loss of Life and Property

Stubbornness can cost loss of life and property, as it happened to king Pharaoh, his warriors and his chariots at the Red Sea. Even before the episode of the Red Sea, many lives were lost through the plagues while livestock and agricultural resources were wasted, just because of one man's stubbornness – king Pharaoh!

In the same vein, a stubborn fornicator may meet with sudden death. In some African culture and magic, there are evil powers that can make such a man somersault immediately after committing the act and die, leaving the woman to wriggle in shame for the rest of her life. In some other cultures, the woman will die during labour if she fails to mention all the names of men who have had sexual affairs with her.

Disease

Sometimes, stubbornness can cause disease, as it did to king Uzziah who ended up with leprosy and was therefore isolated from the people, from his family, loved ones, and from all comforts of life for the rest of his life - 2 Chronicles 26:16-19.

Nowadays, some deadly and shameful diseases afflict people who stubbornly indulge in fornication. Sexually transmitted diseases are increasing every moment. AIDS is the most recent of them all.

Affliction

Stubbornness may lead to torture and afflictions. This was the case of Samson who never desisted from following strange women despite the advice and warnings of his parents, until he ended up losing his two eyes and becoming a grinder in the prison and a mockery to the Philistines.

King Uzziah never knew that God had great numbers of invisible angels assigned to guard and minister to the Church: *"And to the angel of the church of Smyrna…to the angel of the church of Pergamos…angel of the church of Thyatira write…"* – Revelation 2:8, 12 and 18.

Angels are powerful supernatural beings. Can anyone withstand the angel of the Lord in battle? Jacob tried it and he limbed for the rest of his life! Only one angel smote one hundred and eighty five thousand (185,000) soldiers to death in one night during king Sennacherib of Assyria – 2 Kings 19:35. Again, one angel of the Lord smote King Herod to death for out-stepping his honourary boundary – Acts 12:23. Similarly, only one angel massacred seventy thousand (70,000) innocent people because of census stubbornly conducted by David – 2 Samuel 24:2-4 and 16.

CHAPTER SIX

THE MAN UZZIAH

Uzziah means different things to different people depending on the aspect of his life one considers. When viewed from the positive aspect of life, the personality of Uzziah as well as his performance portrays the following enviable qualities, which no one would want to die.

One: Uzziah, a God-bearing Name

Uzziah means *'the Lord is my strength'*. The name one bears, they say, usually has significant influence over one's life. Thus, the strength of God was evident in the life of king Uzziah as the Lord made him prospered and had victory over all his enemies during his time until he trespassed against the Lord. The Bible says the Lord never faints or gets weary but strengthens the faint. Therefore, His strength is enough to preserve and sustain a person until the end of life journey as long as the person trusts in Him. The presence of such divine strength would guarantee victory over life issues and obstacles. No one would love such a man to die because of many benefits that could come from him.

Two: Uzziah, a King

Uzziah was a king. Kingship is a position of honour, dominion, authority, power and influence that everyone would love to attain in life! After all, not all the children born into the royal family can become a king but only the first son – if death permits. Uzziah was therefore, lucky to mount the throne as the first son.

The king was the highest position in the land at that time – the equivalent of Governor or President of our present days. The king reigns and rules over his subjects and until the king dies; nobody can fill that exalted position. At such an exalted position, no king would want to die, no beneficiary would also pray for his death. If the king is godly and is a blessing to the citizens, majority of his subjects would wish him a long life. Even, where the king is tyrannical and becomes a curse and sorrow to the people, those that benefit from his rulership would not want him to die. Who is the king over your life?

Three: Uzziah, an Achiever

Uzziah had a lot of achievement for which he could be remembered namely; invention of war engines for successful battles, military security and safety, building of towers in Jerusalem and deserts and re-building of walls of Jerusalem that was broken down during his predecessors – 2 Chronicles 25:23. Uzziah did not only break the records set by his predecessors, he also benchmarked some records for the successors to follow. Definitely, nobody would like such an achiever to die because he has done good things which the people can remember him for. What can you be remembered for?

Four: Uzziah, a Prosperous Man

He was a prosperous king. The prosperity was directly from God whom he sought in his early reign: *'the Lord prospered him'*. He was successful in virtually all his ways and endeavours. Therefore, the name Uzziah means 'prosperity in the godly way'. Such level of prosperity cannot be exhausted by the immediate family but shall go down to generations to come. No one would want such a prosperous man to die in the family. To them, Uzziah must live on.

Considering the outstanding qualities mentioned above, it may be unreasonable for anyone to pray that **'Uzziah must die'**. This will amount to killing one's destiny with one's own hand. It means killing a king, a good starter, an achiever and prosperity. Definitely, such prayer would seem to be out of tune. The song and tune would rather be: *'all hail the king, long live our king'!*

The Other Side of Uzziah

There is another side of the personality of Uzziah and his principle that portrays an entirely different picture that warrants that he should die. Though Uzziah was a king with honour, prosperity and a lot of achievements but his life ended in sorrow, shame and trauma. According to Jesus, 'what shall it profit a man to gain the whole world and lose his soul?' – Mark 8: 36-37.

One: Uzziah, a Stubborn Man

King Uzziah represents stubbornness. The preceding chapter showed how stubborn king Uzziah was when he insisted on burning incense amidst all persuasions. He held on to what did not belong to him until he lost what belonged to him. He was bent on his action until the action bent his life beyond recovery. He was stubborn to commit spiritual illegality, to refuse warnings against impending danger of that illegal action and his stubbornness made him end up a leper, rejected, disgraced, dethroned and substituted. Therefore, stubbornness, which Uzziah represents, must not thrive in one's life but must die!

Two: Uzziah, a Bad Finisher

Uzziah is a symbol of somebody who started well but ended ingloriously. According to the Bible, *"better is the end of a thing than the beginning thereof: and the patient in the spirit is better than the proud in spirit"* – Ecclesiastes 7:8. He was a man who fell out of the grace of God due to pride and, in spite of all his achievements, prosperity, fame and efforts; he ended up in shame, ridicule and rejection. He became a bad reference point for leprosy in the history of his royal family. Nobody wants to end up the way king Uzziah did. Therefore, whatever would make one finish the journey wounded, defeated and hopeless must die!

Three: Uzziah, a Proud Man

Uzziah represents **PRIDE**. The Bible says Uzziah's heart *was lifted up*. He became proud unto God and unto the priests who customarily anointed him with oil into the royal position and office.

Evidently, pride destroyed everything the king had achieved in life - wealth, fame, ministry, vision and dreams. He enjoyed the morning and afternoon of his life in splendour but spent his nighttime in sorrow and shame. The king lost the glamour of the position and power that once intoxicated him. Pride raised him high up and later dumped him into a deep pit where he could not lift himself up again. What a sorrowful experience he had with pride! Should such Uzziah – pride - continue to live?

Four: Uzziah, an Angry Man

Uzziah was an epitome of **ANGER.** Anger did not allow him to respect the presence of God and His priests in the holy temple. The Bible says, *"be not be hasty in thy spirit to be angry: for anger resteth in the bosom of fools"* – Ecclesiastes 7:9. Hence, anger made a fool of the king.

Anger is demonic and can be inherited. People born into the families that worship *Ogun* (the god of Iron) or *Sango* (god of Thunder) usually inherit anger as behaviour. They are easily provoked and, in the heat of their anger, they can kill and destroy lives and properties. The spirit of *'ogun'* and *'sango'* are in control of their lives. Anger controlled the life of Uzziah and he was thrown out of the presence of God. The same anger controlled the life of Moses and he missed the Promised Land of Canaan for which he had labored for 40years. Should the spirit of anger continue to live in us and make us miss heaven? Surely, that Uzziah must die.

Five: Uzziah, a Leper

Uzziah becomes an epitome of **LEPROSY.** This is the penalty for his pride, anger and stubbornness. He was stricken with leprosy and he became a rejected, disgraced and sorrowful person for the rest of his life!

The Bible records that leprosy even rose up in the forehead of the king and as a leper; he was thrust out of the temple, house of prayer, house of refuge and out of the presence of God who he once sought! - 2 Chronicles 26:19-21. He was cut off from the source of life and light and from all divine blessings. What a bad way to end a life!

Leprosy is a disease of shame and dishonour. Amazingly, God knows how to deal with a stubborn and proud person in order to humble him. He made leprosy to come out *at the forehead* of king Uzziah, at the very point where crown or cap could not cover! He could not hide or deny it because it was open for the eyes to see.

Today, many people have become spiritual lepers due to sin and have been cut off from the Lord: no dream, vision, revelation or voice any more. Sin is a spiritual leprosy that has no medical cure except cleansing by the blood of Jesus. Should such Uzziah continue to live on? Surely, Uzziah and everything he represents must die.

Six: Uzziah, a Loser

Uzziah started a good race but lost in the end. He started with wisdom but ended in foolishness. He started with humility but ended in pride. He started with the fear of God but ended in stubbornness. He started with sound health but ended with leprosy.

Finally, as a leper, the king forfeited his position while still alive and another man was enthroned in his stead: *"and Jotham his son was over the king's house, judging the people of the land"* - 2 Chronicles 26:21. He achieved a lot but in the end, he lost all – position, authority, wealth and enjoyment. What a trauma and psychological torture! The king probably lost the kingdom of God because it was not on record that he repented. What does it profit a man to gain the whole world and lose his soul?

The Consequences of letting Uzziah live

The consequences of letting Uzziah live are many.

One, it can cause *irreparable damage* to one's life, name, career and future. It is worthy to note that when Uzziah was stricken with leprosy, his physical body became diseased, his joy cut off, his relationship with people became repulsive and he was physically cut off from position as king.

In like manner, people stricken with evil because of bad action such as abusing the elders or servants of God, committing adultery, fornication and abortion, usually live scattered, battered and unsettled lives. Their lives never recovered from the ruins that resulted from such evil strike.

Two, it can cause *psychological disorder*. For the rest of his life, Uzziah definitely lived with psychological torment, demoralization, shame and stigma. A man once living in the affluence of the palace ended up is living a solitary life in a self-confined prison. What a traumatic experience!

Three, it can cause *loss of position and authority*. Uzziah lost the kingship position that was once intoxicating him. Likewise, Judas Iscariot, Demas and Gehazi lost their positions as Christ's disciples because of **covetousness, love of money** and **betrayal.** Any action that can truncate one's life must be avoided.

Four, it can make one *to lose heaven*. Pride, anger or disease that Uzziah represents, is the property of Satan and is not strange to the people of the world. In fact, it is their way of life. By pride, Satan lost heaven forever. By anger, Moses failed to reach the Promised Land of Canaan. Likewise, whosoever commits these things will not be fit to make heaven – Galatians 5:20-21.

As for Christians, the Bible advises us to watch and pray that we enter not into such temptations. We are to *'lay aside every weight and the sin that doth so easily beset us'* – Hebrews 12:1. They easily and subtly enter into believer's life and feature at a time least expected, thereby causing some great and irreparable damages.

What doest it profit a man to gain the whole world and lose his soul? All achievement, progress, wealth or prosperity on earth without making heaven is like a race that never finishes well and strong. Therefore, all forms of Uzziah: Backsliding, Pride, Anger, Stubbornness, Disobedience and the rest of them must die in your life, home, and society before you can see the glory of God. This was what happened to Prophet Isaiah, it also must happen to you.

God is not against the good things of life for man but He gives preference and priority to man's soul over the goods of life. What does it profit a man to gain the whole world and lose his soul? What can a man use in exchange for his soul? There is no achievement, position, power, or wealth….that must make man lose his life to hell fire or take over the place of God in one's life.

However prominent or negligent, honourable or disgraceful, good or bad, great or small, admirable or despiteful, famous or irrelevant, high or low, a thing may be, nothing should be able to separate us from our eternal Rock of Ages. All wealth, position, silver or gold will be left behind when we die and leave the world, then man will wake up to judgment before God to determine where to spend the eternity. Abuse of wealth or position will end up in hell.

In summary, to let Uzziah live;
- Is to start a thing and never end well.
- Is to start a journey and never finish strong.
- Is to acquire great wealth and never enjoy it.
- Is to end up isolated in life.
- Is to be dishonoured by man and rejected by heaven.
- Is to be barred from coming to the presence of God.
- Is to be disgraced out of the presence of God.
- Is to probably end up a leper.
- Is to become ridiculed in the end.
- Is to be rejected here on earth and in the last day.
- Is to end up in the bad side of life.
- Is never to realize the fulfillment of one's good dream.
- Is to be dead while living.

MUST UZZIAH DIE OR LIVE?

CHAPTER SEVEN

UZZIAH IN THE LIFE OF ISAIAH

The man Uzziah and what he stands for will not be complete without particular reference to the great vision which prophet Isaiah saw after the death of king Uzziah. The prophet declared that; *"In the year that king Uzziah died I saw also the Lord sitting upon a throne, high and lifted up, and his train filled the temple"* - Isaiah 6:1.

This declaration is a food for thought and needs to be properly digested. Some people saw this declaration as an ordinary statement that referred to a particular date, time and period of event but to some schools of thought, the declaration seemed to carry some spiritual weights. Although there was no elaborate biblical records to show what actually transpired between the king and the prophet, a peep into the life of prophet Isaiah before and after the death of king Uzziah revealed some spiritual truth that is worthy of note.

Before Uzziah Died

The relationship between Prophet Isaiah and King Uzziah was an intimate one and undoubtedly cordial.

One, Uzziah was the natural and physical king over prophet Isaiah. Isaiah was the son of Amoz and a famous prophet of God in Judah and Jerusalem during the reigns of five different kings; namely, Uzziah, Jotham, Ahaz, Hezekiah and Manasseh. He lived around 700BC and started his prophetic ministry probably few years before the death of king Uzziah. In those days, the prophets used to anoint the kings for enthronement. Therefore, there existed some kind of cordial relationship between the kings and the prophets.

More so, a king has influence, authority and dominion over his subjects – land and people. The prophet probably allowed the influence of this mortal king to override the kingship of the immortal king of Israel! This surely blindfolded the prophet from seeing the glory of God as long as Uzziah lived. Who is king over your head?

Secondly, Prophet Isaiah was a close relation of king Uzziah. According to the tradition of the Jews, Isaiah's father, Amoz, was believed to be the brother of Amaziah, the father of king Uzziah. Suffice to say that prophet Isaiah belonged to a royal lineage and therefore had easy access to the affluence of the palace. The blood affinity and family tie is usually strong and that would not make it easy for the prophet to contradict any evil decision or action of the king.

Thirdly, the names *Uzziah* and *Isaiah* sounded alike and had the same origin. Uzziah means '*the Lord is my strength*' while Isaiah means '*the Lord is salvation*'. These common features could generate a strong bond and interest between the king and the prophet.

Fourthly, Isaiah was probably a spiritual adviser to king Uzziah because, in those days, the kings relied on the prophets of the land to get divine direction from God. Therefore, both king and prophet have complementary functions and roles for the peaceful co-existence of the people.

The Life of Prophet Isaiah After Uzziah Died.

One: **Prophet Isaiah was able to see the vision of the glory of the Lord.**

The prophet saw the vision of the Lord and declared; *"In the year that king Uzziah died I saw also the Lord sitting upon a throne, high and lifted up, and his train filled the temple"* – Isaiah 6:1. The inference here is that the king constituted a spiritual blockage to the prophet when he was alive. The relationship and palace romance did not allow the prophet to have total dedication to the service of the Lord. His service and obedience were partly to God and partly to the king. In Matthew 6:24, Jesus said it was not possible for anyone to serve two masters with equal satisfaction. Hence, his vision was limited to earthly sphere - Judah and Jerusalem, for example.

After king Uzziah died, the spiritual blockage seemed to be removed and prophet Isaiah was able to see the heavenly beings as well as hear the voice of the Lord: *'Also I heard the voice of the Lord, saying, Whom shall I send, and who will go for us? Then said I, Here am I; send me'* Isaiah 6:8. This brought about the life-transformation experienced by the prophet during and after the vision. The vision also provided insight to some basic requirement, truth and understanding for our Christian living and ministerial experience.

Two: **Isaiah experienced Divine Discovery and Purification.**

The prophet was able to discover he was a man of unclean lips after the death of king Uzziah. All he could see before that time was the sins and filthiness of other people, making him to preach *woes* to them, inviting them to come and reason with the Lord for forgiveness, and cleansing. However, when Prophet Isaiah discovered his spiritual infirmity, he made personal confession and the Lord forgave him his sin and purified him with burning coals of fire. There is need for spiritual discovery of oneself so that one can make corrections. This is possible only when one has a personal encounter with God.

Today, many people suffer the same fate like prophet Isaiah without seeing the need to discover, recover and purify themselves. Their lips have become unclean with curses, lies, slandering, backbiting, devilish songs and praises, food sacrificed to idols, vain vows and promises; and using of satanic lipsticks in the name of fashion and civilization. Sermons from such unclean lips cannot change the life of the congregation positively however powerful they may be.

Beyond this, many people have unclean eyes, ears, heart, marriage, business, wealth, ministries. In essence, there is uncleanness all over the place – in the family, church, society and nation. The need for spiritual sanitation now becomes imperative.

Discovery of oneself in the mirror of the word of God and taking a step of recovery through repentance is in line with bible doctrine. This is the work of grace available in Jesus Christ only through his blood that was shed for the remission of our sins.

Unfortunately, many people never found time to see who they really were in the mirror of the word of God. They went to church only to see the *speck in the eyes* of other brethren but failed to see *the log in their own eyes.* Until you see, you cannot discover and until you discover, you cannot recover.

Even when they eventually discovered their own uncleanness, they never surrendered themselves to the Lord for purging and purification due to pride and arrogance. They towed the line of pride and anger, just like king Uzziah, instead of bending down with humility to receive grace like prophet Isaiah.

UNTIL YOU DISCOVER YOU CANNOT RECOVER

Three: Isaiah Received a Second Call into prophetic Ministry

Besides the general call unto salvation (which is the first call), there is usually a second or specific call into the following ministries: Apostles, Prophets, Evangelists, Pastors and Teachers – Ephesians 4:11. It is usually a call for the purified heart and ready vessel. Moses, Samuel and Paul heard this specific call and this was why they flourished excellently well in their respective ministries.

Prophet Isaiah heard the second call while he was worshipping the Lord in the temple with full concentration and there was no Uzziah to divert his attention. *'Also I heard the voice of the Lord, saying, Whom shall I send, and who will go for us?'* - Isaiah 6:8. Unlike some calls, which would require the interpretation of a spiritual father like Eli to Samuel and Prophet Ananias to Paul, the call of the Lord to Isaiah was very clear, plain and direct and, therefore, there was immediate positive response: *'Then said I, Here am I; send me'* - Isaiah 6:8.

Unfortunately, today, many people never heard a second call before dabbling into ministry. They called themselves into it because of their bellies and for financial gains. Even when they heard, worldly affairs would not allow them to respond on time.

Four: Isaiah obtained a new Commitment, new Commissioning and new Message.

God's call requires some level of commitment. Isaiah, who had probably been working partly for himself, partly for king Uzziah and partly for God had now received a new and total commitment to go and work for the Lord and to work according to His divine will and purpose: *'Also I heard the voice... Whom shall I send, and <u>who will go for us?</u>* Isaiah now seemed to realize the new commitment as he answered: <u>*Here am I; send me*</u>' - Isaiah 6:8'.

Apart from the general mandate for all believers to preach the gospel to all nations in Matthew 28:19-20, there is usually a special commissioning (the spiritual authority) needed by one to go into the ministry. The Lord commissioned the prophet afresh saying, <u>*'Go, and tell this people....'*</u>- Isaiah 6:9-10. The word *'go'* is a divine command.

Furthermore, divine call is always accompanied by divine message when all necessary spiritual processes are completed. For example, Moses received a message of salvation and deliverance to the people of Israel who were under the captivity of Egypt: *'let my people go'* – Exodus 2:10, 5:1. Apostle Paul was given a gospel message to the gentiles.

Likewise, Prophet Isaiah received a specific message from the Lord to tell the people: *'Go, and tell this people, <u>Hear ye indeed, but understand not; and see ye indeed, but perceive not'</u>*. Who can declare such tough message except God sends him? The later chapters of his book contained the prophetic messages about salvation through Jesus Christ.

Unfortunately, today, there are a number of ministers of God without specific message to specific audience and who never received formal commissioning before they launched out to the ministerial field. Heaven would not back such people up. This is because before the Lord commanded someone to *'go'*, he had already gone ahead of him to clear the way. Such ministers go about pirating messages and sermons of others. They have no specific ministries but operate in any area of ministry that seems to be the order of the day. No wonder they resorted to un-godly powers to perform miracles!

Five: Isaiah Understood That Somebody Or Something Needed To Die.

Prophet Isaiah was able to see a divine revelation or vision **'after the death'** of Uzziah. This suggests that somebody or something needed to die in one's life before one could see divine revelation, move to the next level, or have breakthrough, progress or victory in life. For example, Hamaan had to die for Mordecai to attain the position of favour and authority – Esther 8:2. Likewise, Moses had to die before the mantle of leadership could fall upon Joshua while king Pharaoh perished for Israelites to survive the captivity of the Egyptians - Exodus 14:28.

In similar manner, king Uzziah died before God was revealed to prophet Isaiah. Until the earthly king dies, the heavenly king may not be revealed.

> # UNTIL EARTHLY KING DIES, HEAVENLY KING MAY NOT BE REVEALED

It is not necessarily a person but something so precious must die, or be forsaken or removed out of the way for someone to make progress in life. That is, separation is necessary between you and somebody or something for you to take your rightful position in life.

For example, *SIN* must die in one's life to enable one enter into the glory of God, enjoy divine visitation, and receive anointing for the work of the Lord. In Romans 7:21-25, Apostle Paul had to fight sin and flesh to death before he could become a successful minister of the gospel.

Unfortunately, today, pride, egoism, self-importance, self-acclamation, fighting, stealing, lying, backbiting, drunkenness, smoking, malice, fornication and all forms of wickedness are still much alive and active in many professed Christians. The old man, the Adamic nature, is still much alive in them. They are yet to put off the old man and put on the new man, which is Christ Jesus. They are not yet crucified with Christ. *What has died in your life?*

Six: Isaiah experienced True Worship of God.

When king Uzziah died, prophet Isaiah was able to worship the immortal king with full concentration of body, soul and spirit. As a result, the prophet was able to see and know the following attributes of the Lord:

One: **The Lord is everlasting.**

Though king of Israel dies but God of Israel lives forevermore: '*I saw also the Lord sitting upon a throne, high and lifted up, and his train filled the temple*' Isaiah 6:1. When king Uzziah was no longer on the throne, the prophet still saw the Lord sitting on the throne. God never dies!

KINGS OF ISRAEL DIE
BUT
GOD OF ISRAEL LIVES

Two: **The Lord is supreme.**

The Lord's throne was *high and lifted up.* This shows that the Lord is supreme and is lifted up '*far above all principality, and power, and might, and dominion, and every name that is named, not only in this world, but also in that which is to come*' - Eph 1:21.

Three: **The Lord is holy.**

The Lord's *'train filled the temple'* and the Seraphims were shouting: *'Holy, holy, holy, is the LORD of hosts: the whole earth is full of his glory'* to confirm the holiness of the Lord. The Lord's train is amazingly large because the longest wedding gown ever known does not go beyond the sitting coverage of the bride. This means people who stand in His holy place should keep the house of the clean and tidy and they should be holy, having *clean hands, and a pure heart* - Psalm 24:4.

Four: **The Lord is awesome.**

The Lord is fearful. The Seraphims had to cover their faces with their wings; they could not behold His face - Isaiah 6:2. Fear God and keep His commandment: for this is the whole duty of man – Ecclesiastes 12:13.

Five: **The Lord is merciful.**

The Lord is merciful. Whoever humbles himself before him and confesses his sin, he will show him mercy. As the prophet confessed his uncleanness, the Lord declared *'Lo, this hath touched thy lips; and thine iniquity is taken away, and thy sin purged'* - Isaiah 6:5-7.

It is very clear from above explanation that prophet Isaiah saw the glory of the Lord and underwent a spiritual surgical operation that transformed his life and ministry after king Uzziah was out of his life. He was able to give full concentration to the service of the Lord without any distraction or side attraction from the king. With this, the prophet had his spiritual eyes opened to see the invisible and his spiritual ears opened to hear the inaudible and he was able to proclaim God's message like never before. It could therefore be right to say that the presence of Uzziah in one's life constitutes strong blockage to one's heavenly vision, fulfillment of dream and aspiration, blessing, glory and destiny. Such Uzziah must die.

Chapter Eight

UZZIAH IN OUR LIVES

I n the preceding chapters, Uzziah had been identified, analyzed and presented in terms of personality traits some of which could obstruct the manifestation of the glory and power of God in one's life. Some of the negative traits, which Uzziah represents, are pride, anger, stubbornness, boundary crossing and leprosy. Beyond these, many other things stand as Uzziah that can obstruct divine programme in an individual life and these things must be dealt with.

Physical Uzziah.

The type of relationship between Uzziah and Isaiah also exist in our own lives today. There are people - man or woman, young or old, whose interplay and romance with our lives have a direct, or indirect, negative influence and control over our progress, destiny or glory.

Like king Uzziah, these people may be close relations, friends, community leaders and spiritual heads with strong connections or bonds to our lives. We put our trust in them and, in most cases, cannot do anything without their contributions, advice or instructions because they know the secret and story of our lives from childbirth. Most times, they make final decision concerning crucial matters in our lives and have made themselves kings and lords over our lives!

Unknowingly to us, some of them are agents of darkness and satanic warlords like Goliath and witch-queens like Jezebel. They consult the deities of the land such as 'Ifa' oracle, masquerades and other idols to foresee our future and glory and make evil covenants and enchantment to block it. They raise satanic altars to exchange the glory of other members of the family with sorrow, ill luck or disease. They can even decide to send a person to early grave without attaining the glory.

Should such Uzziah of a people continue to live?

Satan and Demons as Uzziah.

These invisible and spiritual personalities hinder the glory of God from shining out. Satan is the archenemy and accuser of man. With a network of demons, his assignment is to steal, to kill and to destroy man and his destiny – John 10:10.

Satan, who fell off the position of glory in heaven due to pride, is a glory-destroyer, glory-suppressor, glory-hijacker and glory-hater, and he is ready to trade pride with wealth, position, power and achievement as he did with the Lord Jesus but failed - Luke 4:5-8.

However, his operations and manifestations through the mind, thoughts, and actions can be resisted: *'resist the devil and he will flee from us'* - James 4:7. Believers are enjoined not to have fellowship with them - 2 Corinthians 6:14-16.

Sin or Pleasure as Uzziah

SIN is an invisible gorge that separates man from the glory of God – Isaiah 59:1-2. When sin entered the life of Adam, it broke his fellowship with God, made him to lose the glory of God and then caused him to be thrown out of the paradise-like Garden of Eden.

Sin still hinders man from receiving the glory of God today. Like leprosy, sin causes man to be rejected by God the Creator as well as prevents man from entering the kingdom of God.

Under whatever names and forms, sin has permeated our lives, homes, churches, societies and nations worldwide and it has limited the manifestations of the glory and power of God. Greediness, stinginess, deceit, rebellion, murder and laziness, etc, are among the long list of sins mentioned in *Galatians 5:19-21*. Sin is detestable to God because God is holy. Except sin dies, man cannot see the glory of God. A hymn goes thus:

Holy, holy, holy
The eyes of sinful man
Thy glory cannot see.

Pleasure, when unchecked, can lead to sin thereby causing hindrance to God's glory in one's life. The Bible says; *"but she that liveth in pleasure is dead while she liveth"* – 1 Timothy 5:6.

Religious Uzziah

Traditional or false religions are a form of Uzziah against the gospel. The gospel of our Lord Jesus is a glorious plan, purpose and programme of God for the salvation of man. After the fall of man in the Garden of Eden, man attempted to recover the lost glory by evoking many different religions, sacrifices and offerings to seek God. Many of these religions are idolatry and therefore a terrible sin, which the first part of the Ten Commandments abhorred it and sought to address.

Egypt and Babylon are typical examples of idolatrous nations. During the times of the kings, idolatry became prominent in which altars were built in high places all over the place. Even when Christian religion came on board; people did not want to change from Judaism to Christianity because of the physical gains obtained from the old religion:

"...But because of the physical gains derived from sacrifices in the first religion, people refuse to surrender to the better Covenant of the gospel" - Hebrews 8:7.

Today, the worship of gods and goddess such as *Ogun (god of iron), Ifa oracle (divination), Sango (god of thunder), Osun (river goddess), Yemoja (queen of the river)* and masquerades are some of the popular traditional religions in this side of the African world and they serve as Uzziahs to the propagation of the of the gospel. Every traditional religion is associated with series of taboos and superstitions that harden the heart of the unbelievers from accepting the gospel. These religions have their own celebrations and festivals that accrue physical gains to their adherents. Therefore, the people counted the gospel as a new religion and a threat to the existing traditional religions and their numerous benefits.

Furthermore, there is evolution of modern religions, which blend truth with philosophy and demonic doctrines, aimed at sweeping people off the right path of God. These religions are full of heresies and not founded on the foundation of the apostles and the prophets. They are on personal and self-thought ideologies as well as demonic visions from the cosmic world. These religions spread fast and are gaining grounds today far beyond the gospel. However, the Bible alerts and warns us against these false religions in the end time, which is now - 2 Peter 2:1-2.

Therefore, Satan, sin and traditional religions have covered the earth and the people with darkness thus preventing the people from seeing the glory of the Lord but the good Lord has commanded Christians to arise in the light of the gospel of Jesus Christ and shine.

'Arise and shine.....darkness shall cover the earth, gross darkness the people: but the glory of the Lord shall arise upon thee, and his glory shall be seen upon thee' – Isaiah 60:2.

Unfortunately, today, the more we preach the gospel, the more people run into ungodly religions in search of power, position and wealth. Why is this so? Because, the original message of salvation, which is repentance, sanctification, holiness has changed to message of prosperity, success, victory and anointing. Notwithstanding, we must arise to eradicate ungodly religions. How can we do this?

We must arise to PREACH them to death.
We must arise to PRAY them to death.
We must arise to LIVE them to death.

Chapter Nine

UZZIAH MUST DIE

As mentioned in previous chapters, Uzziah is somebody or something, which constitutes an obstacle to the progress, success or glory of another. Such thing should die and get out of the way. There are ways to deal with the Uzziahs of our lives, society and the gospel.

One: Preaching Uzziah to Death.

Our Lord Jesus was quite aware of the state of darkness that covered the people hence the Great Commission is essentially *'preaching the gospel to every creature'* – Mark 16:15. He even gave us the power of the Holy Spirit to do this – Acts. 1:8. According to the words of Jesus, the core of the gospel is repentance: *'repent; for the kingdom of heaven is at hand'* – Matthew 4:14. The gospel is preaching against the spiritual Uzziah of sin, Satan, self and traditional beliefs so that people will turn away from their evil, sinful, idolatry and traditional ways of life and come into the marvelous light of God – 1 Peter 2:9.

Jesus preached Uzziah to death.

Jesus Christ went about preaching and teaching the word of God so powerfully that the hearers described Him **'as one having authority'** – Matthew 7:29. Multitudes would gather round him as they received salvation, healing, deliverance and miracles from the bondage of Uzziahs of sin, sickness, and diseases through his preaching.

In those days, the Pharisees, Sadducees and the Scribes were strong physical Uzziahs to the preaching of the gospel. People looked unto them as the custodians of the law. They upheld the Old Testament religion and would do anything possible to oppose Jesus in the public. They did not accept the gospel because it would erode them of the physical gains they derived from the old religion.

Worse still, they would discourage other people from believing the preaching of Jesus even when glaring miracles did occur! How did Jesus tackle them? Jesus preached them to a corner one day. He preached against their hypocrisy by crying seven big *woes* against the Scribes and Pharisees - Matthew 23:13-36. The woes were intended to put to death the opposition, which they mounted against the gospel of truth and life.

Furthermore, during his earthly ministry, Jesus moved from village to village, across social and cultural barriers to preach the gospel. He later commissioned all the believers to do the same – Matthew 28: 19-20.

Apostles Preached Uzziah to Death.

Apostle Peter was one of the disciples who preached the gospel powerfully with the help of Holy Spirit. On the day of Pentecost, his powerful preaching broke the hardened heart of spectators and 3,000 souls were released from the cover of darkness unto the light of salvation– Acts 2:41. At another occasion, about 5,000 people believed and accepted the gospel – Acts 4:5.

Apostle Paul was another powerful preacher of the gospel. He was once a strong Uzziah of the gospel, persecuting Christians, before he had an encounter with Jesus on his way to Damascus – Acts 9:3-4. When he became converted, he began to preach the gospel of Jesus, which he once opposed - Acts 9:20. And when he was imprisoned by the other Uzziahs of his time, he wrote down his messages as epistles and sent them out to be preached in all the churches. The word of God was not bound – 2Timothy 2:9.

The prayers and messages of Paul went a long way in spreading the gospel of Jesus to even our present generation. While prayer alerts the heaven, preaching alerts the hearts of men. Faith comes by hearing – Romans 10:17. Hearing the gospel being preached will change the heart, the ways, ideas, visions and missions of the people.

In his numerous preaching, Paul exposed the secrets of powers of darkness and the fierce judgment of God that await them. People must be able to differentiate between the light and darkness, the benefits and the disadvantages, both now and hereafter. Paul preached to the Gentile world because thick darkness of idolatry covered them. Thank God, we have the gospel in this side of the world today. It is our duty to preach it to every nook and cranny of our regions.

> # PRAYER ALERTS THE HEAVEN
> # BUT
> # PREACHING ALERTS THE HEART

Apostle Paul preached the gospel with such great power that the people of Ephesus brought out their magic books and burnt them publicly – Acts 19: 19. In other words, he preached to death the long-standing tradition (spiritual Uzziah) in the land as the people accepted the gospel of Christ. No wonder Paul cried out, "*woe unto me if I fail to preach the gospel.*" This is because he saw the gospel as the most powerful way to change the society and even the whole world over. In fact, that was the allegation of the religious Jews against them.

> # THE LONG-STANDING TRADITION OF
> # EPHESUS WAS PREACHED TO DEATH.

Demetrius, the silversmith, accused Paul of preaching against man-made gods thereby making him lose a lot of profit as well as making the goddess Artemis to lose her dignity – Acts 19: 26-27. This means that Paul was not afraid to preach down the gods and goddesses of the land. He surely preached the Uzziah of the gospel to death in that city!

In his preaching, Paul did not mince word in speaking out against sin and all forms of bad characters. He preached a lot on Christian living in the church, home and the society. Christian virtues such as holiness, love, obedience, humility, submission, etc, are a few of them.

Believers must preach Uzziah to death.

How would the people hear the gospel if there were no preachers like Paul who realized the urgency by which the gospel must be preached?

People are lamenting in sorrow and hardship today due to ignorance of God's salvation plan and programme. There are still people like Cornelius who are still doing things in the old, wrong way, in the name of preserving the tradition of the land. We need people like Peter who can reach out to them with the gospel, otherwise, darkness will continue to live in them and with them, and even spread to others.

Likewise, many people like Saul need to encounter the light of the gospel so that they also can become Paul for the sake of the gospel. Hence, there is need for all believers to arise and shine the light of the gospel wherever we find ourselves. We must preach darkness down. Superstition must die! Uzziah must die! The glory of the Lord must become clear for the people to see and behold.

Two: Praying Uzziah to Death

When the early church encountered strong opposition, persecutions and destabilization from the Uzziahs of her own time - the Jewish religion and its adherents, the Pharisees and Sadducees, the apostles accompanied their preaching with the weapon of prayer in order to have breakthrough and to overcome.

Jesus prayed Uzziah to death.

The role of prayer in the preaching of the gospel cannot be underrated. Our Lord Jesus started his earthly ministry after a forty days fasting and prayer in the wilderness and he continued in prayer and numerous night vigils on the mountains as long as the ministry lasted – Matthew 4:2, 17. This gave the Lord victory over all the Uzziahs that rose up against the gospel – the human, spiritual and religious Uzziahs like the Pharisees, Satan, demons and Judaism.

The Apostles Prayed Uzziahs to Death.

It is not out of place to note also that ten days marathon fasting and prayer session preceded the Pentecost before they received empowerment – Acts 1:13-14. After the Pentecost, the apostles continued the preaching of the gospel in serious prayer for them to overcome persecution, intimidation, imprisonment and killing that arose against the church and the propagation of the gospel – Acts 4:24-31, 6:4.

The Early Church Prayed Uzziahs to Death.

Satan and the host of darkness, in order to cover the gospel, raised human Uzziahs, powerful men, even kings like Herod to persecute the church and the preachers but the glory of God still shone for the people to see. The Bible records that Herod died but the gospel began to spread – Acts 12:24. Prayer is an effective weapon against Satan and the host of darkness when applied in the following ways.

First, **prayer must be consistent before and after every preaching exercise.** One cannot successfully carry out the Great Commission without wrestling against the devil who is the prince of this world. It is worthy to note that, having lost the battle against Jesus Christ, the devil has resolved to wage war against them, *'which keep the commandments of God and have the testimony of Jesus Christ'* – Revelation 12:17. Here, we can see that the devil is out to attack the hearers, the listeners, the keepers and the preachers of the gospel. Therefore, constant prayer should be raised for all these sets of people.

Secondly, **prayer must be fervent and powerful.** The word of God that we hear will have positive effect only when we powerfully pray it down our lives. It can be a personal or corporate prayer but must be powerful. The early church devoted their time **'continually to prayer and to the ministry of the word'**– Acts 6:4.

Like in the case of Peter, we need a powerful corporate prayer today to open all spiritual prisons and break the satanic chains on the gospel and the preachers and to silence the stubborn Herod advocates.

By powerful prayer of forgiveness offered by Stephen, the first Martyr, Saul of Tarsus who once persecuted the church a great deal, interestingly, did not die physically but received conversion from Saul to Paul, from a sinner to a saint, a persecutor to a propagator of the gospel. Better still, the Uzziah of pride and persecution in him died he became the **Uzziah turned Isaiah!**

> # BY PRAYER, SAUL OF TARSUS BECAME PAUL – AN UZZIAH TURNED ISAIAH!

Powerful prayer must be prayed - the type that can rain down fire and thunder upon idolatry as in the days of Prophet Elijah – 1King 18. God will not tolerate his children to worship or serve any other gods or idols – Exodus 20. Hence, he commanded the Israelites to wipe out all forms of idolatry whenever they got to the Promised Land of Canaan.

THE DEATH OF UZZIAH DOES NOT NECESSARILY MEAN PHYSICAL DEATH BUT SEPARATION BETWEEN YOU AND SIN, SELF, SATAN AND TRADITIONAL RELIGION.

If the Lord Jesus could pray powerfully throughout his ministry, the Bible enjoins us to pray without ceasing – 1 Thessalonians 5:27. Powerful prayers should be directed toward appropriate targets i.e. against the devil himself and all his agents. As Paul often requested, we should pray for the preachers as well as for the people. Such prayers tips are listed below.

- God should crush every satanic workforce on assignment against the gospel.
- Pray against every religious demon on assignment.
- That every closed door against the gospel to open – 1 Corinthians 16:9.
- God should open the doors to the hearts of the people.
- God should smash every satanic gate mounted against the gospel.
- Every satanic altar already put in place to collapse.
- That the blood of Jesus should neutralize every ritual or sacrifice performed against the gospel or the preacher.
- That the word of God should not be bound – 2 Tim2:9.
- God should give unction and anointing to the preacher.
- Thunder should crash down every evil satellite.
- God should paralyze all evil monitoring spirit.
- God should remove satanic veils from the eyes and mind of the people.
- God should break and soften every stony heart.
- The Holy Spirit should empower the word for penetration into the ears and hearts of the hearers.
- Pray against the spirit of error – pulpit error, preaching error, etc.
- Pray for a balance preaching.
- Pray for strength to withstand and overcome temptation.
- Pray for boldness and wisdom for the preacher.

Three: Living Uzziah To Death.

The ultimate purpose of preaching the gospel is to make the people change from their old sinful ways of life to a new life of the gospel. Preaching and praying alone may not exterminate the Uzziahs of our lives and that of the gospel. There is a need to live what we preach and pray. Our ways of life, walk, talk, work and dressing should convince people of other faiths that we are truly born again, and are followers of Christ. The Bible says we are the light and salt of the world. The importance of salt and light in anything cannot be overemphasized. Wherever we find ourselves, people should be able to see in us the truth, faithfulness, honesty, dedication, holiness, humility and all godly attitudes.

Jesus lived Uzziah to death.

Jesus lived a holy life throughout his lifetime such that the prince of this world found nothing against him - no sin, no selfishness.

The Apostles lived Uzziah to death.

The disciples in Antioch lived the gospel life to the extent that the community identified and called them *'Christians'* – Acts 11:26.

Paul made it known that we are the epistle that people do read – 2 Corinthians 3:2. We are a peculiar people, and the society expects from us a higher standard of living – a high level of morality, no compromising deal, integrity and love of neighbour. Our lives should be able to challenge the unbelievers. Paul struggled very hard to live the gospel way. At first, he cried out *'the good I want to do I cannot do but the evil I hate I still do, who can deliver me from this sinful flesh'*. Later, he was able to say *'I have fought a good fight, I have finished my course, I have kept the faith'* – 2 Timothy 4:7. This means he had not only preached the gospel but he had also lived according to the gospel and he became a challenge to the Pharisees, his old folks.

Moreover, Apostle Paul forsook many of his rights and benefits in order to gain Christ. He lived a life worthy of emulation and was bold to ask people to follow his example – 1 Corinthians 11:1. His epistles contained tonic for practical Christian living, which were borne out of his experience.

Jeremiah was another man who preached and lived according to his preaching, his persecution and imprisonment notwithstanding.

Believers must live Uzziah to Death.

Is your behaviour in line with the Bible teachings? Is the word of your mouth seasoned with salt or is it just another sharp and poisonous sword? Perhaps you keep bad company; this will corrupt your good manner and therefore throw you out of God's circle.

The Bible teaches obedience, submission, hospitality, humility, holiness, etc. Can you score yourself a mark on these? The dos and don'ts of the Bible are for our strict observance; what is your percentage of compliance?

In a very clear language, we are enjoined to be the doers of the word and not only the hearers – James 1:22, 25. Therefore, let us cultivate to live what we preach or profess. People of other faith are watching us. Our enemy, the devil is also roaming about seeking whom to devour. He can only get hold of those who fail to live according to the word of God.

Living the gospel is an automatic way of executing Uzziah of sin and tradition to death but it requires a lot of self-sacrifice, suffering, commitment and endurance. We need to observe the word, meditate on it and do it before we can enjoy the blessing and prosperity of God that has no sorrow attached – Joshua 1:8.

King David expatiated more on how to make the word of God our way of life. According to Psalm 119:1-18, the bible enjoins us to *keep, walk in the law, keep thy testimonies, not wander from* all point out to living by the word of God. Verse 17 says it more clearly; 'that I may *live* and *keep* thy word'. Verse 13 says, 'with my lips have I *declared* all the judgments of thy mouth'. *Declare* here means to *speak* or *preach*. Therefore, as you declare and live by the word of God then you are indirectly preaching and living Uzziah to death!

THE CONCLUSION

Uzziah, as described, discussed and explained in this book, are those things that can block your way and efforts to glory and divine placement, however beautiful, comfortable and approachable those things may appear to be. Uzziah may either be human or spirit being. In the journey of life, one is bound to meet different types of Uzziah on the way. What then should one do?

Already, fierce judgment has been passed against Uzziah - Satan, sin, self and ungodly religions. It is the verdict of destruction and eternal death.

Sins of pride, anger, fornication, adultery, idolatry and wickedness are products of Satan. Whoever trades in them has been judged to end up with Satan in hell fire! – Revelations 20:10-15.

Therefore, 'Uzziah must die' is a:
- ❖ Divine verdict already passed against Satan and sinners.
- ❖ Decree and declaration one needs to make against Satan, sin and self.
- ❖ Decision to make if one must get to heaven.
- ❖ Determination that one needs to be able finish the heavenly race to the promised land of heaven.
- ❖ Spiritual warfare that one must fight and win if one must make heaven.
- ❖ Fervent prayer needed by heaven-bound believers.
- ❖ Divine judgment that must be executed speedily – Psalm 149:9.

Spiritual Uzziahs like pride, anger, stubbornness, idolatry, cultism and worldliness, etc, must die through preaching, praying or living by God's word while fervent prayer can incapacitate physical Uzziahs.

Satan has been overcome by the blood of Jesus (Revelation 12:11) and can be resisted by quoting the written word of God (James 4:7).

Sin cannot die but one can be dead to sin and exercise dominion over sin through the power of Calvary – Romans 6:12-14. Secondly, the word of God contains the dos and don'ts of life, which guides us against committing sin. The word is our life (Deuteronomy 32:47) and we should read it, study it, and meditate on it constantly (Joshua 1:8).

Self can be put under control and subjection through fasting and prayer as Apostle Paul did. New birth means becoming a new being, a new nature, a new creature, behold old nature (the flesh, the self) is passed away.

"Thou shall not suffer a witch to live" is the bible verdict against all spiritual wickedness – Exodus 22:18. This verdict applies to human Uzziah who stands to obstruct God's purpose or programme. However, if the human Uzziah has a divine encounter with Jesus Christ and turns to become Isaiah, the verdict may not be executed by the mercy of God. If a sinner turns a saint like Saul turned to Paul, the verdict may not be executed.

It is only God who, in His infinite mercy, who can protect someone against a written verdict. That kind of mercy is available only in the Lord Jesus Christ whose blood speaks mercy and forgiveness for a sinner rather than cry for vengeance like the blood of Abel - Hebrews 12:24. The judgment will only be suspended for any human Uzziah who comes to repentance before he goes to the grave. Otherwise, the verdict is sure for execution!!!